A Dialogue

with Depression
Om Devi, 2017

A Dialogue with Depression
Heart/Mind Disconnect

iUniverse books may be ordered through booksellers or by contacting:

iUniverse
1663 Liberty Drive
Bloomington, IN 47403
www.iuniverse.com
1-800-Authors (1-800-288-4677)

Because of the dynamic nature of the Internet, any web addresses or links contained in this book may have changed since publication and may no longer be valid. The views expressed in this work are solely those of the author and do not necessarily reflect the views of the publisher, and the publisher hereby disclaims any responsibility for them.

Any people depicted in stock imagery provided by Thinkstock are models, and such images are being used for illustrative purposes only. Certain stock imagery © Thinkstock.

ISBN: 978-1-5320-2890-8 (sc)
ISBN: 978-1-5320-2892-2 (hc)
ISBN: 978-1-5320-2891-5 (e)

Library of Congress Control Number: 2017911356

Print information available on the last page.

iUniverse rev. date: 09/14/2017

A Dialogue with Depression
or
Heart/Mind Disconnect

It is unusual that one finds a title first,
but as thoughts flow outward,
feelings are condensed.
Now it is time to make sense of events past, present, and future.

Om Devi copyright 2017

Contents

Preface

A *Dialogue with Depression* took many years to come into being. Throughout the years I wrote down many thoughts since I had no one to share my feelings with about my crumbling relationship with my husband. I finally realized I was part of a repetitive story and wanted to change it.

I realized that others might also get some use from these offerings. We are not alone in our sufferings. We need support.

We watch tides rise up on both sides of us. Here in the middle, with hope, perseverance, and determination, we fight to survive until the end. Here we can accept loss and move on or perish mentally, physically, emotionally, and spiritually.

In compassionate memory of a husband
who did.

Introduction

I grew up in a middle-class family. My mother was always right with no room for discussion. I think this was a cover for insecurity and possibly the beginning of depression. My father was always working and on the road. As it turned out, he also had lady friends on his journeys. After this discovery, years later, my mother was very angry and developed clinical depression.

This was the household I grew up in. I was always trying to make things better for both my parents but never succeeded. After all, I was only a child.

School became important to me, partially as an escape from family. In third grade, I had three amazing teachers who inspired me to become a teacher after I had something to teach. (Yoga and art history were my two gigs.)

In middle school, there was another great teacher who inspired me to write.

In high school, I felt more stifled. Much memorization was needed, and I really had to study to understand why and retain information.

I was determined to succeed in my studies at college. I discovered art history and photography, which became my passions. Photography became my profession.

As a woman was trained in those days, love was far more important than a career, so I got married and moved to be with the man I loved. Because I was in love, my husband's career came first. I accepted this at some level. I worked in photography part-time.

After my husband completed his residency, he became a physician. He listened carefully to patients, hearing things other people had missed. His secondary passion was economics, which got him more involved with economics in medicine. Losing contact with individual people moved him closer to his clinical depression. Long gray winters in the town he worked in was another push towards illness that was undiagnosed. We all assumed he was just a quiet, introverted, shy academic since childhood. This too was an indication for possibilities of depression that no one paid attention to.

He was very studious. He advanced in school quickly and went to college at the age of sixteen. He always told me how frustrated he was because he could not matriculate easily in college. He was too young to enjoy dating and socializing, so he became more introverted and studied even more. Another push.

These are the brief histories of the two characters that create *A Dialogue with Depression*.

In our early years, we enjoyed each other's company, and we would talk forever. We became very good friends. We were very close. We got married.

We found a house close to work. I continued to work in photography. My husband advanced in his medical profession. As I recall, he was always frustrated and never satisfied with how he was treated by his superiors. He felt he was never appreciated enough, which hurt him deeply (another clue unnoticed to underlying depression). He always felt he did not get enough pats on the back at work, so he kept switching jobs, seeking. We moved from here to there trying to find his unrequited praise. He ignored and undervalued the support of his wife. He was very successful at work yet never felt he was good enough because of the lack of praise. Over time his perception of lack of appreciation weakened his spirit and heart. He was seeking the impossible.

He took another job in another cold and rainy city. It was a terrible climate for an introvert and someone who suffered from depression, now diagnosed. I never realized he suffered so acutely from depression because he was so lively at work. His mind took him a long way before it stifled his heart. Again, his illness was ignored. At one point, we moved to a sunny, warm city, which did help lighten his spirits for a while. He actually got into yoga and meditation. His job in the sun was tough because he had to cut unproductive programs for the company. People did not like him for that. Another push toward illness.

Over time I realized that, though he said he worked for both of us, I came in second. This was very difficult for me to accept. It felt like I was in last place and there was nothing I could do about it. Distance, space, and time between us. There was only time for work and very little time for me. His work became an addiction. It probably always was. He was in his own world. He was a man who wanted to become very important in his field. He did succeed at a price—at a very high price that eventually took his life. He separated himself from his wife and family. He worked so long and hard that he lost contact with good health and his wife's strong support.

One day he ignored the flu. He had to work. He got so sick he was hospitalized. He waited too long to see a doctor. Flu affected his heart *(a weak spot for those who suffer from depression)*. He developed atrial fibrillation. He went back to work.

We moved many times for his career. My photography was no longer viable in terms of a career for myself. I got more involved in fine art. I was no slouch when it came to art and cooking.

Art and cooking kept me creative and busy while my husband, addicted to work, continued to have very little time for us together.

He stopped exercising and socializing outside of work. He had no time. He only had time for work. I became an inconvenience.

In my art field, I used yoga to help me center and focus. Through yoga, a practice of medicine from India came to my attention called Ayurveda, which helps balance imbalances. The medical practice of Ayurveda existed in India for several thousand years. It answered questions that I could not get answers for from Western medicine. To be healthy through Ayurveda seemed logical. Health was encouraged through diet, lifestyle, exercise, massage, and herbs. Ayurveda was a preventative and supportive approach to well-being mentally, physically, and spiritually. I was hungry to learn more, eventually receiving my second MA in Ayurveda. (My first master's degree was an MFA in photography.) I developed a client base in Ayurveda and yoga, my new art. It was time to give back. My clients became my art work that I could send home to their families, usually feeling better. This was a wonderful substitute for not having children, which my husband never wanted.

My husband continued to slip more into himself and work. His obsession with work kept him away from home longer and longer, until he was diagnosed with full-blown clinical depression. When he came home, he was silent, gobbled a good meal down, watched TV, and went into the back room to sleep alone. This went on for many years. I was unable to help. He didn't like my telling him truth about his work addiction or depression. He tuned me out. Why would a physician want to listen to his wife?

Unable to offer help, I became frustrated, which moved to anger. I was an outsider. After all the years of proofing his papers and preparing meals for his colleagues, I was no longer part of the family I wanted to be part of. He could not hear information from me or his psychologist and psychiatrist. He manipulated the system in his ill health behavior. He was bright, and he was arrogant. He kept all of us at a distance. He had to work. He had little interest in making friends, with no hobbies outside of work. He only traveled for work. He had no adventures unless I dragged him along. He would write in notebooks, in very small handwriting about trivia he could impress his colleagues with. All therapeutic information he received from his doctors was applied at work, never at home.

With my new studies in Ayurveda, I was able to encourage him to practice some breathing techniques, some meditation, some yoga, and some study in Sanskrit. He also applied these positives to work, not family. He briefly participated in life outside of work because of Ayurveda. Eventually he described this and me as too much trouble. He went back to work. His fatigue increased, leading to more bad health.

This distancing moved me to take notes, write prose, write poetry, write letters, take photographs, write down thoughts, research depression, and find statistics.

I hope some of my observations may allow us to recognize earlier signs of clinical depression and to hear silent cries for help.

I share with you *"A Dialogue with Depression"*.

Trying to Understand ... Not Understanding

There has been a distancing for many tears/years now.
I felt hurt when connection could not be made.
Without connection, I took things personally.

It took many years to understand what was wrong. It took many years to
think I could make things better for us, which I could not make better.
I tried to take things into my own hands, even
though the events were outside myself.
He is the sufferer, and I suffered.

I was an outsider, because of the relationship that had
disappeared into dislocation, disregard, and isolation.
I moved with him from one job to another.
I changed my personality.
I thought about what I had done wrong.
He said it was only himself.
How could that be?

I tried to figure out what was going on.
We stepped further back from ourselves.
We sought therapy, yet only the healthy one heard.
Again, more on my shoulders.
What did this mean?
How could I fix this?

If I could only work harder.
If I could find another way to fix the relationship.
I became more independent.
I could not fix him; I could only take care of myself.
I became more creative. I studied depression through thoughts,
books, papers, physicians, therapists, and articles.
I was in the same story.

He did not change.
He buried himself in work so deeply. He described himself as getting
out of a dark hole every morning until he could no longer get out.

My independence continued.
I put more creativity into my work.
I figured out my mother also suffered from depression, which is
why my mother and my husband communicated so well.

I developed friendships with upbeat humans.
My mate slipped further down the rabbit hole through his
addiction to work, his ego, his looking down upon others.

I thought this must be okay.
I mistook brilliance for arrogance.
More distance.
Many years passed.
I came second to his work and now understand this is reality.

This reality existed for many years of marriage.
He had always denied this.
He said his work was for both of us.

Both of us recognized his work addiction, though he
ignored it and I accepted this behavior.
My anger increased, and he blamed my anger
for his withdrawal from the relationship.
He began to work in a different state.

He no longer came home.
I no longer wanted him to disrupt my life because he only
came home to sleep and stare and be silent.
His depression made him jump into a dark hole,
consuming his once-clear mind and big heart.

Lungs connect with grief.
Liver absorbs anger.
Kidneys hold fear.
Heart is affected by hurt and sorrow.

These relationships find the weakest point in the body to destroy.[1]

---

[1] Studies with Dr. Vasant Lad, Ayurvedic Institute, Albuquerque, New Mexico.

Psychiatrist 1

1992

"He will never change."

I am a strong woman.
I can help.
I can proof his papers to be published.
I can make fine meals.
I can set up a household anywhere he moves us.
I can create a home for him from one coast to another.
I grow older.

This weight of two people gets heavier.

Psychiatrist 2

June 21, 2000

Nearest Relative:
Wife

Appearance and General Behavior:
His dress is neat.
His posture is tense.
His facial expression is sad.
His physical activity is underactive.

Emotional Reaction:
His attitude is reserved, scared, and sad.

His Talk:
The form is logical.
The rate is under-talkative.
The quality is controlled.

His Expressions:
He has suicidal thoughts.

Does the Patient Know Who He Is?
Yes.

Does the Patient Know Where He Is?
Yes.

Date?
Yes.

How He Feels?
Yes.

General Knowledge:
President?
Yes.

Pursuant to the provisions of the law as amended, the respondent was taken into custody by the undersigned and detained for a seventy-two-hour treatment and evaluation at hospital.

Conclusion:
The respondent appears to be mentally ill, and as a result of such mental illness, he appears to be in imminent danger to himself.

Psychiatrist's Notes:
Patient referred to hospital emergency room by psychiatrist.
"Patient has suicidal ideation with plan to drive off mountain road. Has stopped car to look at appropriate ravines. Plans to cut self with knife. Has taken knives out to look at them and held knife to wrist."

Husband and Wife Discussion:
He told me he did this to get attention.
I told him his suicide would cause pain to himself,
me, and his family and friends.
He listened without hearing.
He was numb.
I sought help from family, who thought it must be my
fault. After all, he was a brilliant fellow.
Where was my support?

Treatment:
-Prozac
-Talk therapy
-Darkness revisited
www.depressioncentral.com
(For a man who does not like working with computers, he searches.)
He went back to work.

This was my first introduction to clinical depression when my husband made his first attempt at suicide. This was approximately ten years before his successful suicide death.

This suicide attempt was bizarre. It happened when he was not around me, and I received a call from a hospital where he turned himself in. I was alone. This news put me in shock. I was driving when I received this news via cell phone. I was unable to get other information because the only person who could release the information to me was my husband, who was obviously in no condition to release information.

I walked into the hospital, where I had to be screened via a metal detector to see if I carried potential weapons—weapons like long socks, belts, nail clippers, a nail file, a penknife. These items didn't occur to me to be weapons. I saw before me what was once an animated husband who was now in the throes of Prozac numbness and fog. My shock continued. I was not prepared, and I had no one other than my husband to talk to—no one to discuss him with or share the shock. He had moved us again, so I had no close people to share with. I never thought of signing up with a therapist before, never thought I needed one.

I was okay.

Finally, there was some coherency, and this man, my husband, who I thought I knew and loved, could talk. He said, "I did this to get attention." What was this? *Wow*, a cry for help. He cut his wrist with a paring knife? This was why the suicide attempt was not successful. He was looking for help. He did not want to kill himself.

Finally, after days of him being dazed, I received permission to meet with his psychiatrist. I could sit in on a meeting! I watched a discussion between the psychiatrist and my husband. I listened baffled, shocked, confused. I thought this must be a dream, better described as a nightmare. I thought this man was strong and brilliant. I didn't have a clue that suicide was a possibility.

He came home, still under the influence of drugs. He lost his ability to feel and work through issues he had with himself or me. He was numb. The medicine helped block emotions, so he could exist and go back to work, not allowing the patient to discover what moved him to this state.

I had an idea I thought might help. Unfortunately, this came from a point of my not understanding the disease, the medication, or the clinical depression. I was not part of this because I did not have this illness. I was healthy.

I spoke to him from my perspective. I confirmed he was asking for help. I asked which knife he took from the knife set. Again, I never thought of these as weapons, just tools for chopping, cutting, and slicing food for a wonderful recipe. The brand-new, expensive set we had invested in were not weapons for destruction. He showed me he used the paring knife.

I told him to take this knife and break the blade in the driveway and bury it. I thought this could represent burying the incident and the pain. I talked to him about how much pain he had caused me and his parents, how much sadness this had caused me, and how much his death would have created great tragedy in the family. I thought he heard. Again, this illness did not allow for social consciousness and understanding. He was unavailable. He could not understand the feelings of someone outside himself. He could not see how this violent action to himself could affect his wife and other people who cared about him. This verbiage did not register. There was no connection.

This was the sick mind, the illness. Depression is so self-involving that the person suffering from it cannot understand that this violent act not only affects himself but others. Committing suicide affects all of his friends, his relatives, his colleagues. It sends shudders through the entire community. The illness numbs him to this awareness of affecting others. The medicines he was prescribed numbed him for months. He had no interest in talking further. He had no interest in any physical relationship—no holding hands, no hugs. He was no longer present outside of work, where he gave the greatest performances of his life. He had a glimmer of awareness about health when I began my studies in Ayurveda and he attempted yoga and meditation for several years, which did make him more social at home.

Again, clinical depression took over.

My observations of his clinical depression:

- Stage 1: His studious childhood—isolation.
- Stage 2: College and early career—continued isolation.
- Stage 3: His inability to combine work with marriage until his first suicide attempt—inability to understand emotions.
- Stage 4: Control with exercise and diet and intervals of medicine.
- Stage 5: Overwhelming issues from the disease stops him from remaining healthy.
- Stage 6: Achieves his end game of death via successful suicide.

(After his first attempt at suicide, I waited days, months, and years
for that other shoe to drop. One cannot help but wait for the
next event, hoping it will never happen. Somewhere in your heart
and mind and soul, filed deep down inside, you still wait.)

May 16, 2000

Dear husband

I want to be with you so badly, and yet because you won't really address the issues I need addressed, I can't be close to you. You must really get some help so you actually understand what I am talking about, because I don't see any resolution until then. Speaking to a good therapist will make you understand how to respond to what I need, and this isn't just a selfish matter. It will make your spirit rise. It will open your heart to help you in everything you do. You will find peace, strength, time to do things you want and inner strength to take on the sorrows of the day.
I see you as a nut (seed) locked in a shell. You have closed yourself off within your own walls and stopped sharing love and joy. May you find the soil to nourish yourself and make you open up and grow into a warm, healthy sapling.

Love,
Wife

Dearest husband,

You have presented me with a most difficult task that becomes necessary for me to do. This note comes from the bottom of my heart with more love for you than you may never know. It is time for you to step up to the plate and take that scientific step, that leap of faith. If you really love me, love your work, love your family, love you, it is your time to show it. You must understand with all of your mind and heart *what you must do.* Do not delegate. Do not ignore. Do not pass off. You must show your stuff by understanding others and rising to their needs. It is a large task that you may not know how to do yet. Your safety nets are gone. It is up to you alone to succeed in what you want to succeed in. You can become great because of who you are and what you are capable of becoming. Along with fear, take positive steps now in understanding others (for them, not for your advantage) and fearlessly answer questions about why you really do the things you do. If you really want to get better, it is you who must take this on all by yourself, using the tools others have generously given you for so many years. You must know the success as a physician you are in *your capable hands* to succeed or fail. The knowledge you have received over the years will guide you to success if you use this knowledge wisely. Our relationship's success is in your *capable hands and heart* if you allow all that has been given you to enlighten you and give back with true love, selfless love. Your life is in *your capable hands* if you choose to live it with kindness, gentleness, caring, and loving yourself and others. Your lifestyle is in *your capable hands.* Choose where you really want to live. Do it. Now is the time to act. I have nothing further to add until you know what you want to do and how you want to live and smile with others. I am off. Much love, my darling husband. I pray for your success.

Wife

Here is a Series of Thoughts Written Down

Old age is watching the gleam disappear from your lover's eye,
when touch is an effort and tenderness is washed off shore.
Effects that assure but do not appease.
Ahh,
touch,
the magic that withered
as winter years move
one to learn how to live with loneliness.

Misunderstood

Brilliance for arrogance.

Strength for addiction.

Spaces so wide we can breathe.

We can hear the air under the wings of ravens.
Earth shows us art forms we could never believe true,
and man makes his mark.

(Written in 1999)

Away,
far away,
yet communication is always near.
How strange we are.
Where do our comforts lie?

Suffering

Arrogance versus brilliance.
Power versus truth.
Drugs versus enlightenment.
Me versus we.
I versus divine.
Aged fear versus fearless youth.
Silence versus thanks.

Fighting for immortality is our human bondage.

Not being heard causes illness.
Being alone versus independent makes us fragile.

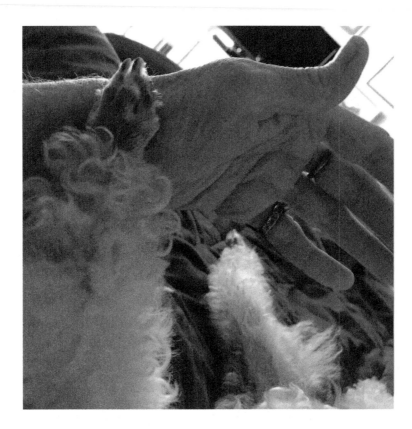

Everyone has different strengths and weaknesses.
With a little patience, there is kindness.

In the land of innocence, before I actually had a head-on collision
with depression, I truly believed we all had the capability to be
happy. These tools are not available to those who suffer.

No matter who we are or where we are
or what we are
or why we are,
we have skills to be happy or not.
We have received a gift,
roots of strength for well-being.

And so this outsider continues to peel back the skin of the sour cherries of pain.

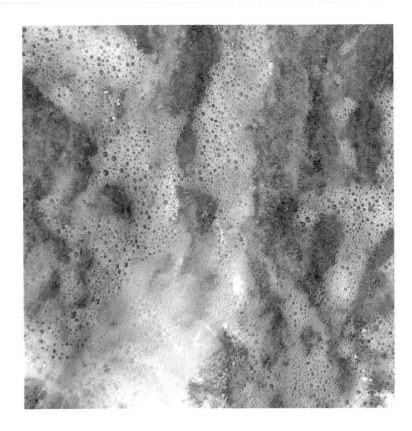

His Letter

(This was a handwritten letter on yellow lined sheets of paper with minimal punctuation. I discovered it in his accounting book where he kept records for taxes. I found this note when he was out of town. This attempt was not realized.)

Dearest wife,

My entire life has been spent cultivating an image of intellectual brilliance that has been fed by my own interior drive that has focused all of my energies on this image and by my ability to suck energy from those around me. This single focus has led me to shortchange those around me, especially you. I can no longer sustain this effort and my arrogance in focusing my life on this image. It has finally become so clear that I cannot ignore it. I have come to my end as I have lived alone, isolated in my mind. You are the person who has been closest to me and has sustained me, but I have not supported you. It has been a one-way street. I cannot ask you to forgive me for my actions, since they are not forgivable. I can only thank you for the thirty-six years of comfort and support that you have given me and for always standing by me, even when you were in great pain because of my actions. I only wish I understood my hated arrogance sooner before it destroyed me and your happiness. I have driven to the overlook to be joined with the ocean.

Husband

Living in the moment allows us to evolve.

Earth
Water
Fire
Air
Space
are what we are made of.
The balance is ours to work with.

Our safety net is knowing we are not alone.
We are enveloped in everything.
We are part of everything.
We are in everything.
We take comfort in this knowledge.

Compassion emerges from wisdom.
Understanding flourishes.

I always felt as if I was on the periphery, watching.
I was not aware of my value.
I became an observer who stopped observing myself.

As dewdrops turn to tears of changing seasons,
winter captures them and turns tears into diamonds.

There is a fine line between greatness and madness.
Perhaps the difference between the two is the ability to take on responsibility.

Her heart cries out for herself.
She had accepted it is acceptable not to be heard.
It was okay to be ignored.
The good child told the bad child,
beaten then forgiven.
This parent training allows unacceptable actions to happen and be forgiven.

She feels fragile. She has to let go of taking care of each other.
She realizes she has to take care of herself.
She learns protection is when something doesn't feel good, she shouldn't do it.
If something is too difficult, she is tired and doesn't want to fight.
She must give herself permission to let things go.

My life progressed.
I tried to be a chameleon to fit in.
I tried to reinvent myself to be with someone.
This time I reinvented myself again,
but this time it was for me.
It is difficult to get over memories.
I must leave some behind.
This time tears and laughter are mine.
I am who I am, like it or leave it,
with love and compassion for myself.

When he is depressed,
she finds it very difficult to understand.
She takes his actions personally.

The relationship gets confused with lack of
understanding of this debilitating illness
and the suffering he is going through.

The combination of the depression and work
addiction increases effects of the illness.

November 11, 2013
A phone message left on my cell phone.

Husband
Wife, right now I feel completely dead inside from the depression, both
about the money and just how I feel and how afraid I am for the future.
I know—I agree with you.
I am not treating you well.
I am not disputing that.
But right now I am struggling to survive,
and I am giving it all I've got.
You are a great person, not a bad person,
obviously.
Obviously, you never have done anything to deserve this,
and it's grossly unfair that it has happened to you,
but I am trying to figure out what I can do about it.
I am sorry I did not come straight to you,
that I thought I was going to meet you and didn't talk to
you about it first before I launched myself off.
I am sorry I am in such bad shape,
and I am sorry you got stuck with me.
I am sorry I cannot deliver what you need at an
emotional level and a physical level,
and you have every right to be mad and upset.

October 2013 until August 2014

Text messages.

The dialogue continues.

I sent this text to his Western health practitioner.

Wife
Observation:
He is suffering in acute stage depression,
fear,
anxiety,
being incapable in decision making,
insomnia, and
suicidal thoughts.
I have not seen him in three months.
He is very involved in work out of state.
His response to depression is work addiction.
He is not responsive to me.

The allopathic physician wants to place him on medication.
It is difficult to watch someone you have been with for almost thirty-seven years have a Band-Aid put on a symptom rather than finding root cause.

The doctor scheduled an appointment.

Wife's E-mail to Husband:
Her heart aches, and nausea goes to her gut.
She is in deep grief and sorrow about a relationship she thought would not
end if both parties tried to show and express love toward each other.
Neither can see that expression of love from each other.
Then he took a job in another state and just left her.
He said he loves her.
He faded out of the relationship slowly.
Then he just stopped coming home.
No holding.
No loving.
No kind words.
He just left.
She stayed away to sort things out.
Nausea and pain comes in waves.
Her dogs comfort her and kiss her tears rolling down her cheeks.
The man she thought she knew for forty years is gone without
a trace of love or friendship or kindness—no effort.
No white knight, no last-ditch effort.
He stays at work.
Her heart is broken.
She can't believe this.
Why?

Husband
Silence.
Wife's Thoughts
She feels his fear resonating from him in cyberspace.
There's clearly no trust.
Disbelief.
Positive thoughts change to negative.
After all these years,
wow.
A human so paralyzed.

Therapist
Realization often comes with an unexpected bolt that often makes us stronger.
Stay with truth. This is no time for expectations.

Wife Texts Her Husband, Again

Because of his distancing over these months (his choice),
he avoids personal holidays.
She sees no closeness.
She no longer has an interest in having him walk the dogs.
She no longer has an interest in cooking or cleaning for him.
She is capable of doing her own marketing.
Her needs that he knows is buying her olives!
She finds it difficult to watch him take over space or withdraw completely.
She cannot be comfortable in his presence.
He cannot make amends at a social level.
She no longer has the energy to carry him.
He has taken thirty-plus days off from work and has no interest in seeing her.
He mentions a visit Thanksgiving weekend.
She thinks of all the preparation necessary for someone
who will not be present and who will return to work.
He does not show for a time to help restore the relationship.
She did not want him to ruin a national holiday
memory with his suicidal thoughts.
Perhaps he should visit his brothers and sister instead.
She no longer has the energy to carry him.
He wants to downsize to a small one-bedroom
apartment where he works out of state.
His choice makes it
clear he has no interest in having her there.
When there is no crisis, he says, "I," "I," "I."
Now in crisis, it is "we."
Before downsizing, she asks him to speak to his boss, ask him for help,
perhaps have his boss pay for her to visit him if he is so exhausted,
renegotiate his contract.

Husband
Silence.

Husband
He is concerned about paying out of his retirement account for taxes.
He says all the retirement money will be gone.
If this problem is not fixed, we will have nothing to fall back on.

*(All of this not hearing and no response is odd. Rational
decisions are no longer coming from the man I loved. All of
this is coming from the disease of clinical depression.)*

Text message dialogue continues:

Wife
Why did you cancel Ayurvedic treatment?
Concerned.
Calling the police to see if you are okay.

(Wife receives an annoyed phone call.)

Time passes.

Wife
Plane on time.

Wife
Landed.
Wearing polka-dot jacket.

Husband
Just got off freeway.

Wife
Okay.

Wife
My prayer to you each day is to be happy.
Each day be grateful.

Wife
Found my birthday present.

Husband
What store is this?
Where is it?
*(She offers information. He does nothing. He
misses another of his wife's birthdays.)*

Wife
I am on plane. Looks like departing on time.

Husband
Glad we could have hot chocolate together.
Have a safe flight home.

Wife
Thank you for treating me to hot chocolate.
You were on the cell phone.
I had a hot chocolate.
You had a hot chocolate
My prayer to you each day is to be happy.
Each day be grateful.

Husband
I have landed in Chicago.
Are you home yet?

Wife
No, in air. Many delays.

Husband
Are you there yet?

Wife
Just landed.

Husband
Good. Glad you made it.

Wife
(now paying bills)
Need charge card clarification. What is FT?

Husband
Subscription to FT.
I called to reverse it.
I should know on Monday or Tuesday if it will be.

Wife
Why cancel?
You love that paper.

Husband
No response.

Wife
All I wanted from you was to hold me and comfort me.
Did not realize it costs so much in your mind.

Husband
No response.

Wife
All I wanted from you was to hold me and comfort me.
Did not realize it costs so much in your mind.

Husband
No response.

Wife
All I wanted from you was to hold me
and comfort me, I did not realize it costs so much in your mind.
This seemed like such a simple concept to me.
You can't even call regularly, not that this is a substitute.
You actually used to call regularly.
I just can't understand any of this.
I don't know how someone dies inside and can be so successful at work.
I guess you can't understand even in my frustration I needed
love and understanding and holding from you.

*(The wife just did not understand this lack of response was due to
his illness. She took this personally. She did not understand.)*

Husband
No response.

Wife
Resends.

Husband
No response.

Wife
Resends.

Husband
No response.

Wife
Resends and resends and resends.

Husband
No response.

Wife
I guess I am exhausted because I have tried so hard for two people and failed.
You don't even tell me about work, what the hotel was like,
what you ate, who you are hiring, why you are hiring?
This all leads to not knowing.

Husband
No response.

Wife
Really?
Forgot you have nothing to say to me anymore.
Really?
After thirty-six years?
You can't even respond?

Husband
No response.

Wife
By the way, this info is an offering of help to get you back.
You don't respond.
You don't want help.
Please don't rely on the feeling that no one gives
you answers, suggestions, wisdom.
The issue is this is not what you want to hear, and
you ignore the ways to take action.

Husband
No response.

Wife
I guess this is it.
I get it.
Goodbye.
*(She didn't get it. It was not that she was being ignored, or that
there was a lack of love. This was his clinical depression.)*

Wife
Just checking, are you calling at 2:00 p.m. my time or your time?

Wife
Surprised you did not call back as you said.
Hope you are feeling better.

Husband
No response.

Husband
The car looks cool! Thank you for the picture.
(Referring to a car rental.)

Wife
Please send me your current biweekly pay statement that includes deductions.

Wife
Ironic you are so eager because you had to wait
nine months for him to be hired at work.
That certainly trumps thirty-six years for me.
How little I am worth.

Husband
No response.

Wife
Did you receive my message about pay statements? Please respond.
Let me know when you will send.
Respond!

Husband
No response.

Wife
Respond so I can release this from my mind.

Wife
Thank you for your response.
(He finally sent statements.)

Husband
No response.

Wife
My sadness is you had to go elsewhere to work.
Much love, health, and joy.

Husband
No response.
(This inability to respond was due to the fatigue of clinical depression.)

Wife
My dream was for us to share adventures and sit at home appreciating
each other and reading comedies and sacred texts together.
I am saddened you have lost this understanding of us
and as in your quote, "I am too much trouble."
My wishes are simply for your healing so you may be happy and
in your right mind. This is so difficult for me because I am so deeply
devoted to you and you are so deeply devoted to work.

Wife
The Ayurvedic treatments you have gifted me were of a great help.
Thank you.
In the past you responded. I hope you are being taken care of.

Husband
No response.

Husband
I am glad the Ayurvedic treatments have been a great gift. I am not
being taken care of. I am struggling to take care of myself. I know that
you are devoted to my welfare and feel deeply for me. I have been
meditating on all you have done for me over the years—the moves,
the meals, the support for my work. I feel deeply that I have failed
to understand and support you at the level you have needed. This
saddens me greatly because this failure is my responsibility alone. I will
love you forever. No one could ever take your place in my heart.

Wife
Nor you.
Love is included in devotion.
I am sorry your guilt is so deep that you find me too difficult
to deal with because I want to be in your life.
It was not all bad. It is just that this past year the negatives greatly outweighed
the positives, and there was no interest in discussion, compromise, or change.
Am I too much trouble because I am a reminder of growing older?

Husband
No, you are not too much trouble. I am diverted from healthy activities by
my concern about money and economic survival in a very hostile world.

Wife
This is a false concern from illness.
One needs very little if one is at peace with one's self.

Wife
I am waiting for your call.

Husband
Will call around four thirty or five.
Just finishing errands.
Need to eat.

(He never called.)

Wife
There is only one person trying here.
Enough is enough.

Husband
I hope you get some rest today and recover from your trip.
Thinking of you.
Sweet dreams.

Wife
Very sick chest.
Have to work today.

Husband
Did you catch a cold?

Wife
The Ayurvedic treatment released deep sorrow and grief.

Husband
July 2014
Dear wife,
I made it to my Ayurvedic treatment this week. I had a private meeting with the doctor today and discussed both my depression and our relationship issues. I would like to discuss this with you. I know you are still recovering from your trip. What would be a good time to call you tomorrow?
Love,
Husband

Wife
(He never made time for this discussion.
He went back to work.)

Husband
I made it to the airport.

Husband
I made it to the connection.

Husband
I made it to the apartment.

Wife
Happy to hear you are safe.

Wife
Look—I know I am not a priority. Just call or text every day from
work to let me know you are among the living. Thank you
Please acknowledge you received this message in a timely fashion.

Wife
Guess you still must be out enjoying the long weekend.
Glad you are having fun.

Wife
Guess you really don't understand.

Husband
I am at the office safely.

Wife
Thank you.
The memory clinic called. Call back.

Husband
I am at the office safely.

Wife
Thank you.

Husband
I made it to the apartment safely.

Wife
Thank you.

Husband
Dearest wife, good morning. I am at the office safely.

Wife
Good morning. Thank you.

Husband
I made it back to the apartment safely. Have fun with your friends.

Wife
Really lovely women.

Husband
Good morning. I made it to the office safely. I am
glad that you had a good time last night.

Husband
I made it to the apartment safely.

Wife
Every day is not the same. These bits should be shared in a relationship.

Husband
I slept in.
Checking into bathtubs now.
(She requested him to check on tubs for a new apartment.)

Wife
Thank you.
I actually think you like feeling sorry for yourself
more than you like me or anyone else.

Husband
Good morning. I do not feel sorry for myself. I feel trapped by my bad
decisions and am trying to come to terms with them every day.
I made it to the office safely.

Husband
I worked late and am safely at the apartment.

*(These short answers were trying to comply with my requests of
communication. With his clinical depression, this was the best he could do.)*

Husband
Good morning. I made it safely to the office for early calls to Europe.

Husband
I worked late and made it back to the apartment safely.

Wife

I am really disappointed with you.

It amazes me that you are so insensitive.

If your routine changes, advance notice is nice so I am prepared for you coming home later, especially when I have to go to bed early for my early day at work.

Is this your anger? Is this just you hating me?

I feel like a mother or a teacher something you force me to be because of your lack of love and compassion toward me.

I deserve at least this consideration. You can put me in your calendar, yet you continually express this bad behavior.

This is exactly what brings on my anger.

One week you can be kind, and the next week you disappear.

I cannot bear this roller coaster of insensitivity and lack of compassion and love.

Husband

I am sorry. I was working on preparing for the BOD meeting and worked late to do so. I forgot that this was your early night because of class tomorrow morning. I want to come see you at the end of next week.

Am I welcome to come?

Wife
My nieces are in town, and I am busy on Wednesday and Thursday.
Planning in advance is useful.
Perhaps another time on neutral ground.

(This happened to be his birthday. The last two years he did not
acknowledge our anniversary or my last two years of birthdays.)

Husband
I am working in the apartment this morning.

Husband
I made it to the office safely.

Husband
I am going to a BOD meeting now at a downtown restaurant. I will
let you know when I arrive at the apartment this evening.

Wife
Thank you.

Husband
I am safely at the apartment. Dinner at cafe downtown. I had kale Caesar
salad, halibut with vegetables, and a variant of strawberry shortcake.
Sweet dreams.

Husband
I am safely at the BOD meeting on the seventy-
fifth floor of a downtown office building.

Husband
I made it back to the apartment safely.

Husband
I made it to the BOD meeting safely.

Husband
I am at the apartment, exhausted after the BOD meeting. I will call tomorrow.

Husband
I have been making calls to Europe this morning at the
apartment and am going to the office now.

Husband
I made it to the office safely.

Husband
I made it back to the apartment safely. I am making dinner and
going to bed early. I hope you and the dogs are safe.

Husband
I made it to the office safely.

Husband
I made it to the apartment safely. I know you have an
early day tomorrow. I hope you sleep well.

Husband
I am working at the apartment.

Wife
Congrats on another year!
BTW, good wishes from your sister-in-law. "Tell him happy birthday!"
Did you just stay at your apartment today?

Wife
Thanks for your immediate response.

Husband
I stayed in to rest. How is your client?

Wife
Badly injured, with lots of fractures and swelling.
It's funny, but in spite of all the pain, he said this was the best thing
that ever happened to him because it brought his family closer
together with a more serious understanding of mortality.

Husband
I hope he recovers without further complications.
I am concerned about his flying after his collapsed lung.

(When it came to work modalities, he was able to briefly
come out of his presentation of depression.)
Wife
He is thinking of flying.

Husband
I would think this trip is dangerous.
I am at my office working today.
Have a great day.

Wife
Got some of his swelling down in his ankles.
Ayurvedic massage training is amazing.

Husband
Just got back and had a late dinner. I am glad that you are able
to help with your skill. I have an early call tomorrow morning.

Husband
I had my early call and made it to the office safely.

Husband
I made it back to the apartment for an early dinner. I
have to review the submission later tonight.

Husband
I made it to the office safely. I'm still working on the submission.

Wife
Wishing you success.

Husband
I made it back to the apartment safely.

Husband
I made it back to the office safely.

Husband
I made it to the apartment safely.

Husband
I made it to my office safely.

Husband
I made it back to the apartment safely. I was excited by your idea
when you called. I am sorry you changed your mind about the trip.

Wife
I did not change my mind. You were ambivalent, and I needed
a definite answer, not, "That sounds interesting."
Stop the games.

*(This was my expression of frustration toward my
husband who presented with this illness.)*

Husband
I am resting at the apartment.

Wife
I just couldn't live in sadness, though I am sad sometimes,
at which point I have to pull myself somewhere to be with
people or take the dogs on a walk to check out wildlife.
It saddens me you don't have an interest to wake up next
to someone to say, "Good morning, I love you."
It sickens me that for so long I had a false hope of enjoying this sort of
relationship with you and tried so hard to have this. I thought you wanted
this too, and I inflicted these needs on someone who has no interest in this.
It is difficult for me yet necessary to move away from this
husband, the beloved physician, because every day there
is a pang of sadness, knowing I am not wanted.
This is my reality check. Don't say, "I want this too,"
because you don't make this happen.
My reality check is that I am very alone and sad because I am alone.

(I was asking for the impossible due to his illness, and I just didn't know this.)

Husband
I know that I have not been able to give you the kind of attention and love that you need. I think back at evenings of television instead of talking and card games, too much travel for business, and too little travel for pleasure with you, too much concern for what my work colleagues think of me and too little concern for your happiness, too much concern for the outward trappings of what money can buy and too little thought for long-term stability. I think about these mistakes every day and can see no way out of their consequences. I live from day to day as best as I can. I have allowed my mania for professional stature to overwhelm my need for personal happiness with a caring person who was always concerned with my well-being.

Wife
Thank you for acknowledging you have made a choice.
You have chosen work.
I've got it.
It's hard to sink in even if I already knew.
I promise it will.

(This was my response of sadness and frustration and anger to him for succumbing to his illness.)

Husband
I am not making a choice for work. I feel trapped in work with no way out that I can see. I miss you and the life I had with you when we lived together in the same state. That is why I wanted to visit you.

Wife
Visit me? I am your wife. (I thought, I did not say it.)
I will try not to bother you with any more questions or comments.
Thank you for your continued financial support
since long ago I gave up a real income job for you and your dreams.

Husband
I realize that you gave up a real income job for me and my dreams.
These dreams have turned into a nightmare for me. I want to hear
your questions and comments. Please do not stop sending them.

Wife
I'm finished.
A lawyer will contact you.
(I had hoped this would shock him into returning to health—my ignorance.)

Husband
What do you mean about a lawyer?

Wife
If you were so alone, you would have invited me to
your place for special weekends. Stop the BS.

Husband
I made it to the office safely. Did you get what you
needed for the insurance question?

Can you come here for the weekend of August 16?

Wife
Possibly. What is happening?
*(I feared the false hope that this could be or
that he would let me down again.)*

Husband
I am back in the apartment safely. There is no event.
(August 27 is our anniversary.)
I was hoping to spend time with you exploring this area.

Wife
What about the dogs?
Will you be staring at the cell phone all the time like the last visit?
Will there be time to settle things?
Will you answer historic questions without prompting?

Husband
I have not decided where to explore yet. I will not be working or looking at the
cell. I have not thought about details yet. We will have time to talk about things

Wife
Hmmm.
Would this incomplete offering be acceptable at work?

Husband
Just consider it.

Wife
It?

Husband
The trip.

(I would fly into his arms if I knew he would be mentally present.)

Husband
I have been in meetings all afternoon. I will call you around 5:00 p.m.

Wife
Not necessary.
(I was working.)

Husband
I called but could not reach you. I will try again tomorrow.
(He did not call.)

Husband
I am at the office in a meeting. I will call you back as soon as I am finished.

Husband
I am at the apartment safely.

Husband
I am at the office. I have settled the bill for the MRI so
you do not have to be concerned about it.

Husband
I am at the apartment. I stayed in resting today.

Husband
I am at the apartment resting. I have a trip to Boston tomorrow and Tuesday.

Wife
Have fun.

Husband
I made it to the airport safely. We started meetings at ten
and finished at six. It will be a long but interesting day.

Husband
I am taking off now.

Husband
I am at the hotel safely.

Wife
Nice.

Husband
I am at the hotel. I'm going to the meeting soon.

Wife
Do you remember name of mortgage company? A friend needs info.

Husband
Name given.

Wife
Thank you.

Husband
I am at the office safely.

Husband
I am at the apartment safely.

Husband
I am working at the apartment today. I am spending the rest
of the day at the apartment. I hope you are well.
(There was no further mention of the invitation to visit him.)

Husband
I made it to the office safely.

Husband
I made it to the apartment safely.

Husband
I am at the office working.

Husband
I am back at the apartment.

Wife
Not me.

Husband
Where are you?

Wife
Philosophically or physically—ahh, that is the question.

Wife
Question: What do you intend to do with these realizations
you have been having through your meditations?

Husband
Answer: I intend to change my behavior toward you, my family, and others.

Wife
When?
How?
In what order?
Who are the others?
Hope you are feeling better.
Are you taking herbs for your cold?
They are okay to take with other herbs.
Are you at work?
Break the routine.

Wife
Please use this prayer:
May my heart be filled with love and compassion.
May my mind be filled with understanding and peace.
May my hands be filled with selfless service.
May my home be filled with abundance and harmony.
May my life be filled with health and prosperity.
May my inner being be filled with wisdom.
"Peace, prosperity and joy to all!" (Brahma Kumaris).

Wife
How did your session go with the accountant?

Husband

It went well. I am continuing to be worried about money for good reason. Although we have paid each quarter as the accountant said, I could not pay the full amount that I should have, so we are behind for the year. Therefore, we will have to take money out of the retirement account again and then have to pay tax on it in 2014. It is very depressing to see the money we worked so hard for go to the government in taxes, all because of a single mistake we made in 2011 of not holding on to the cash. (This was a reference to buying our house outright, a positive effort.) I am sharing this with you so you have the details you need to understand what is going on. This was the theme of our session: giving you more information so you feel included and valued.

Wife

Get off the house.
You told me to sell the apartment, which was paid for.
The house is mine. You gave it to me as a replacement for the apartment.
Stop trying to make me feel bad about your mistake.
This is what comes of no discussion.
(This house was given to me for safekeeping, for our retirement, since he was not thinking rationally and could create more debt.)

Wife
Your money concerns are not with good reason.
The house is not a mistake.
Are you staying at work for the holidays, including Thanksgiving?
You say you cannot handle anger, yet you prick a wound
until you make it bleed again and again.

Husband
You still do not see the situation by the WMD of 2013.

Wife
I do not understand the initials again, my friend. Full disclosure.

*(Text messages were his only communication toward the end.
He stopped calling.)*

A friend paraphrased a comment by Dick Cavett, who also suffered from depression, that if someone had an instant cure for cancer, the patient would travel to the far ends of the earth; for someone who is clinically depressed, if there were a magic pill to cure depression just across the room, the sufferer would not have the energy to get up and take the pill.

He did not call me this weekend. He did not text me this weekend. I thought I would just let him rest. I would wait until he felt like calling me.

I received a call from his boss Monday morning at seven forty-five. He committed suicide. He hung himself at work.

Excerpts from the Autopsy

The coronary arteries show atherosclerosis with approximately 85 percent stenosis of the proximal right coronary artery and no significant stenosis in all other major coronary arteries. The left ventricle is mildly dilated. The distal aorta shows prominent calcific atherosclerosis with plaques.

This sixty-seven-year-old man who was found deceased in the stairwell of a parking garage died of asphyxia due to hanging. Based on the findings of the investigation and autopsy, the manner of death is certified as suicide.

My husband and I had an injured relationship for many years.
The root cause of depression was never really addressed.
He was a brilliant man living inside his mind.

He worked endlessly on the challenges and discoveries and joys
of work. He laughed and shared and allowed his goodness and
ego to spill over onto others, and he was happy at work.

The appearance of happiness at work was a performance
that consumed all of his energy. This took a great deal
of effort for a man who lived inside his head.

When he came home, he shared his exhaustion with me. He stared
into space and television. He couldn't hear me. He didn't even eat
a well-prepared meal at the dining room table. He sat in front of
the television, gulping down food in silence. There was nothing left
of him to build and develop and maintain a relationship of sharing
and feeling with another human being at an equal level.

For some reason, I accepted this because he said his work was for both
of us. I was sad and ached over this. I thought I had never taken the right
action to bring the joy and laughter and communication with him.

I thought he should communicate at home because he did
at work. He finally told me this person at home was who he
really was. At work, he was just doing good acting.

The pain made me question why I stayed. It was because
of our marriage vows—"till death do us part."

In understanding his death, we need to understand progression of disease.

It begins with stress. If he had only taken time out for a few deep
breaths when he was anxious or sad. He ignored this.

Just do one more thing. Disease escalates into clinical depression.

Events and lifestyle *(demands at work and overworking to please, to
be accepted, to get that pat by his boss)* make this disease flourish.

He couldn't make it stop. I, who did not suffer, said, "Get over
it. Be happy." I did not understand that this was like asking
a diabetic to stop taking insulin and be healthy.

This black hole he was in was like stage IV cancer. The demons of pain
and suffering wipe out happiness and joy. The sufferer learns to isolate
himself to be able to end his pain and suffering through suicide.

I must forgive myself.
I must share.
I must talk about mental illness.
I must listen with love and compassion,
so we all can hear,
so we all can heal.

I couldn't stop it.
I watched.
I begged.
I suggested.
I got angry.
I demanded.
I sought support.
I couldn't stop it.
I watched the downward spiral.
I was helpless.
I felt a sinking pit in my stomach.
I was a witness.
Suicide is not a peaceful death. It is violent, and people
left behind see the violence or its repercussions.

For me, there seems to be so much more.
For him, he had enough.

Sometimes writing thoughts down prevents them from eating away at you.
Depression seems to sever the relationship of heart and mind.
Mind overwhelms the heart.

The memory of his depression and suicide is an annoying hum. With time, the hum is reduced.

Eastern and Western Medical Explanations for Clinical Depression

Eastern medicine (Ayurveda) describes disease progression through six stages. The progression of depression is as follows:

- The first stage is accumulation of depression, where negative thoughts or sad thoughts begin.

- The second stage is provocation, causing aggravation of a site where the negative thoughts get stuck in sadness, creating fatigue, withdrawal, and lies to avoid reality.

- The third stage is spread, where changes move to other tissues. Here the mind consumes or overwhelms the heart.

- The fourth stage is qualitative change, where the aggravation moves to a weakened site, being the heart; the heart closes, and blockage occurs.

- The fifth stage is manifestation, where symptoms of disease can be observed. This is when heart vessels block, especially seen with the blockage of coronary arteries.

- The sixth stage is differentiation, where the disease leads to destruction and alteration of tissue. Here the heart breaks.

The heart attacks itself (heart attack) or suicide.[2] In Western medicine, studies also express clinical depression as a risk factor for coronary artery disease in men, demonstrating clinical depression is an independent risk factor for incident coronary artery disease.[3]

---

[2] Vasant Lad, MASC, *Textbook of Ayurveda: A Complete Guide to Clinical Assessment*, Volume 2, chapter 2 (Albuquerque, NM: The Ayurvedic Press, 2006).
[3] Daniel E. Ford, MD, MPH, et al. "Original Investigation, Depression Is a Risk Factor for Coronary Artery Disease in Men, the Precursors Study," *Arch Intern Med*, Vol. 158, July 13, 1998, 1422, American Medical Association.

Through Ayurveda I also discovered that the discussion of depression
is incomplete without discussing the five elements we are made of:
gas or space, air, fire, water, and *earth.*
Each of us are differently weighted or balanced with more
or less of some of these elements than others.
These elements present variations on depression.
Usually the primary elements are the first to
indicate the imbalance of depression.
When secondary and tertiary elements become involved, the fifth and sixth
stages of disease play out through clinical depression—suicide or heart failure.

Air and Space Depression
too much space creating isolation
fear
self-doubt
insecurity
no delineation
which pushes, crushes individual's true nature

Fire and Water Depression
Self-centered
arrogant
work addiction
piercing
which pushes self and crushes self

Earth and Water Depression
greedy
heavy
stuck
congested
which pushes down through congestive heart failure.

He was made up of the five elements with this variation.
His primary elements were *fire and water*.
His secondary elements were *earth and water*.
His tertiary elements were *air and space*.

From grade school, he could be described with depression
and balance at his primary level of fire and water.
In balance, he was educated, analytical, and brilliant.
Out of balance, he showed tendencies toward arrogance, study
addiction, judgment, and piercing comments and observations.

His last fourteen years expressed his secondary elements of earth
and water. In balance, he could be described as methodical,
patient, and steady. Out of balance, he showed tendencies of greed,
heaviness, being stuck, and congestion (especially in the heart).

The year before his death by suicide, he did suffer from right coronary
artery blockage that was undetected until the autopsy.
His third set of qualities were of air and space. In balance, he
could be described as having expansive thought and creativity.
Out of balance, he was isolated, fearful, and filled with insecurity
and self-doubt, with no delineation in judgment.

He was able to maintain this balanced side at work
but not at home or in his emotional life.

"His illness came from an overly powerful mind. In such an individual, there is over confidence and suppression of emotions and physical symptoms. Even though the person may have severe pain, he does not show it. This person is in denial and this can mislead a doctor and prevent treatment."[4]

"When healthy, the fire element brings joy, happiness, contentment and cheerfulness. When a person laughs his fire element is healthy.

When the fire element is abnormal, there is unhappiness, grief, sadness and depression. Fire governs secretion of neurotransmitters and neuro-chemical synthesis of sensation and perception, which becomes understanding. This understanding is higher Cerebral activity and comes from the healthy fire element. If this digestive fire is low this can become chemical depression."[5]

---

[4] Vasant Lad, MASC, *Textbook of Ayurveda: Principles of Management and Treatment*, Volume 3 (Albuquerque, NM: The Ayurvedic Press, 2012).
[5] Vasant Lad, MASC, *Textbook of Ayurveda: Fundamental Principles of Ayurveda*, Volume 1 (Albuquerque, NM: The Ayurvedic Press, 2002), 87.

At some level, we are the cause of our own suffering,
be it genetics, illness, or personal choice.

The disease progresses through diet, lifestyle, behavior, and genetics.

Improving Communication

Can we listen to the whole story of depression?

Observe.

Self-explore.

Witness.

Listen.
Bear witness.

Many times we hear things that shock us. It prevents us from asking questions that may help us understand. Sometimes when we hear someone who is depressed or is doing something in a different way than we would do, we block.

We stop the conversation because we don't know how to continue the conversation. Sometimes information is difficult to digest, and here we lose the dialogue with depression. We don't have the right questions. We don't have open ears to listen. Clinically depressed people are ill. They are not healthy, so they are different. We are all different from each other. This creates difficulty in hearing because we talk instead of bearing witness.

It takes time to hear information we do not understand or that is incompatible to our own thoughts. This new information takes time to digest and accept. When we do, we discover that both sides have truth and wisdom. We develop compassion and understanding. We must learn to validate others by hearing. We must validate ourselves by hearing.

Truth is truth.

An Outsider's Thoughts on Depression

We can study them.
We can advise them.
We can block them.
We *cannot* remove the dark hole.
Do they have the tools to get themselves out of the dark hole?
Where can they find the tools to rise above or dig out?
We need to get the sufferers of depression to tell us what would
be useful, but they do not know themselves and are usually
paralyzed mentally from the disease of clinical depression.
How can we help them get out of the dark hole, or remove the black cloud?
We should not feel superior.
We don't understand this disease and the pain.
We can only see the surface of their illness.
We do not know depression's depths. If we did, could
we prevent the end stage of depression?
Depression comes from different sources.

There are many different types.

We must recognize this.

It is like discussing cancer. There are so many different kinds of cancer, some
curable, some that can go in to remission, while other cancers are incurable.

We must talk with those that suffer.

We must hear the sufferer.

We must not take this personally but objectively.

We cannot fix this disease.

Only they can heal with proper tools:
Exercise?
Diet?
Lifestyle?
Change?
Therapy?
Herbs and medicines?
They must have neutral ground to express their feelings.

We must try to understand.

Depression is at epidemic proportions. One in four American adults suffer from mental illness. That is approximately 61.5 million people.[6] According to National Alliance on Mental Health, 260 million antidepressant prescriptions are filled each year. The total population in the United States is 321 million.

With little long-term research, scientists explore new methods to tell when patients are ready to go off medication. Reasons for continuing medication reduces the risk of relapse of depression by about 50 percent. With each relapse, the risk of an additional bout of depression increases by 16 percent. Reasons for stopping antidepressant medication is their side effects, like weight gain and sexual dysfunction. Women may want to stop before getting pregnant or nursing. More than 303 million prescriptions were filled for antidepressants and mood-stabilizing drugs in 2014, according to IMS Health, which tracks pharmaceutical sales.[7]

---

[6] *AARP, the Magazine*, September 2015, volume 58, #5b, 48.
[7] *The Wall Street Journal*, Tuesday, March 8, 2016, d1.

Falling down
Is part of life.
Getting back up is living.
—Anonymous[8]

[8] Quotable™ Cards, 263.

The Questions for the Living

How will I get through this event?
How will I continue with my life?
What happens next?
I am older.
My financial situation has radically changed. My
husband was the high-income earner.
I earned monies. He considered my business as a write-off.
I went through tears.
I was frustrated.
I was angry.
I had to move on.
I tried to center myself so I could move, so I could work,
so I could.

My grounding has to happen every day so I can maintain my stability.
My daily routine is thanking the planet for allowing me to be present.
I need to focus on breathing so I can take full,
deep breaths to help calm and center.
Then I must focus on movement to maintain physical
strength, flexibility, and endurance.
Movement can be walking, cycling, stretching, or yoga.
The next focus is on positive affirmations.
Then it is important to keep in touch with friends because sometimes they are
concerned about contacting you, since they too are disturbed by this end.
Friends may not know to how to approach the one left behind, because
they do not want to cause more pain or appear insensitive.
Find support groups, people who have suffered similar
events teach you how to witness and listen.
Get something done each day.
Focus on the positive.
The bad thoughts and bad feelings will soften over time.
Everything takes time.

Depression is treated through psychiatry, medicine, and
psychology, talk therapy, in the United States.

Some medicines are created to block depression and numb feelings
that become trapped in the mind, putting pressure on the heart
until it breaks physically or by suicide, which ends the dialogue.

Suppressing thoughts through medicine is a way one
may continue to function in life or in work.

The blocking of the disease never allows the person who suffers from the
illness to get to the root cause of the illness to help understand him or
herself and undo the weaving of many years or generations of suffering.

The medication allows the person to function at base level.
Epidemic proportions of drugs are being used, shifting society from
truth and compassion to shallowness, numbness, and death.

Therapy is also used. The challenge for the therapist is to translate healthy
action to someone who suffers from the demons of depression.
For the clinically depressed person, being happy is a foreign language.
Movement through exercise is impossible due to
the weights of disease the patient bears.
Breathing fully is difficult because the sufferer feels
he is in a dark hole, an enclosed space.
Discussion can begin to resolve the mental pain. Unfortunately, this therapy
often does not continue to take the individual beyond the threshold
of the dark hole, and the patient falls back in. With understanding of
the individual's issues, there is this momentary exit from the hole.

Then with realization and awareness of how this disease has affected his or her loved ones, the sufferer falls back into the dark hole where no one can reach him or her. The therapist is not capable of jumping in with proper tools to bring them both out.

At this point, the earth closes in, and the person is buried in isolation with suicidal thoughts, using his or her tools to develop suicide into reality.

That is the end game of depression.

Held by the Universe
There is a key factor to joy and happiness. I think
I am beginning to recognize this key.
It is not your fault.
You cannot fix things for other people.
You are okay.
Be kind to yourself.
It is not your fault.
You cannot fix others from the outside.
You are a good person ...
I am a good person.
It is not *my* fault.
We may see things in others that seem to be simple fixes. We must let this go.
Everyone is on their own paths.
We are on our own paths of forgiveness, of love, of life.
I am on my own path.
I am a good person.
I am not to blame.
It is not *my* fault.
I cannot fix someone else.
I cannot take care of someone else who does not want to be taken care of.
I must do unto myself as I do kindnesses unto others.
I am a good person.
It is not *my* fault.
I am not alone.
We are not alone.
When we feel we are alone, we are not connected to the
universe. The awareness and healing come from knowing we are
part of the universe. We hold the universe, and it holds us.

And This Is Not the End

Here I am becoming a person with new responses,
new reactions that help me learn and grow.

I am removing myself from the past, from my husband's ego and
fears, his exaggerated thoughts due to clinical depression.
I am learning the art of understanding so I can lower the volume of the
turmoil of the past. I can move on with my life and live in the present.
It is important to find new relationships with their fresh
beginnings and endings and still remain whole.

We have been brought up with fairy tales with romance and
happy endings. It is difficult to place these fairy tales into reality. But
I do still believe in happily ever living and happily ever after with
lessons learned, with no regrets. It helps to love life in the moment
with compassion and caring, even for *me* this time around.
I will seek kindness. I do love life with friends' love and laughter.
The heart can open again or close, and we have to choose a path.
This is my journey—clearing out past chaos, living
with it, embracing it, and letting it go.

Here goes my giant step now …

It is a happy beginning.
It is time to reach out.

Life is catch and release,
letting go, and receiving.

With thanks and gratitude to many friends who have read and reread my manuscript. I raise my glass to I universe, Jeff who encouraged me to proceed, and so much appreciation to my editors Amanda, Kim and Dana who brought loose thoughts, punctuation and tenses into a book I hope will offer solace and hope.
Om Devi

The author has chosen to center the text, as we should be
centered in our lives to stay healthy and balanced.

CPSIA information can be obtained
at www.ICGtesting.com
Printed in the USA
FSOW03n2304041117
40724FS